small world
Eating

Gwenyth Swain

ZERO TO TEN

For Vinnie, who loves to eat!

To find out more about the pictures in this book, turn to page 22.
To find out more about sharing this book with children, turn to page 24.

The photographs in this book are reproduced through the courtesy of: Stephen Graham Photography, front cover; © Elaine Little/World Photo Images, back cover, pp. 9, 18; IPS, p. 1; © Gerald Cubitt, pp. 3, 20; Sharon Wilharm, p. 4; © TRIP/C.C., p. 5; © TRIP/H. Rogers, p. 6; © TRIP/M. Peters, p. 7; ECLA photo. Used by permission of Augsberg Fortress, p. 8; David Chittennden, p. 10; George Washington Carver National Monument, National Parks Service, p. 11; SeaQuest Cruises, p. 12; © TRIP/F. Good, p. 13; F. Botts/FAO, p. 14; Eliot Elisofon, Eliot Elisofon Archives, National Museum of African Art, Smithsonian Institution, p. 15; Jeff Greenberg, p. 16; WPF/FAO photo by F. Mattioli, p. 17; © Lyn Hancock, p. 19; © John Elk, p. 21.

First published in this edition in Great Britain 2004 by Zero To Ten Limited, part of the
Evans Publishing Group, 2A Portman Mansions, Chiltern Street, London W1U 6NR

Copyright © 1999 by Carolrhoda Books, Inc.

First published in the United States by Carolrhoda Books, Inc.,
c/o The Lerner Publishing Group, 241 First Avenue North, Minneapolis, MN 55401 U.S.A.

A CIP catalogue record for this book is available from the British Library.

ISBN 1-84089-329-X

Printed in China by WKT Company Limited

It's time for breakfast.
What will you eat?

Will you put milk on cornflakes?

Or will you grab something sweet?

Eating can be messy.

It's also fun to do.

Wash your hands. Give thanks.

Then dig into your food!

You can eat at a table,

on the ground,

Or on the run.

But before you can eat,
there's a lot to be done.

Buy food or grow it.

Then, pound it or sort it.

Chop it, then stir it.

Grill it on a fire or cook it in a pot.

Food tastes great – sometimes hot,
sometimes not.

When you share a meal,
you share good tastes and good times.

Sit right down. Take a big bite!

Eating will make you feel just right.

More about the Pictures

Front cover: Two boys in Guyana, in South America, slurp flavoured ice-cream cones.

Back cover: A child from the hills in Tamil Nadu, India, sits down to eat.

Page 1: Two English schoolgirls stop for a spaghetti lunch.

Page 3: For this toddler in northern India, breakfast starts with a bottle of milk.

Page 4: This young girl in Cantonment, Florida, USA begins the day with a bowl of cornflakes.

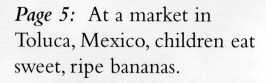

Page 5: At a market in Toluca, Mexico, children eat sweet, ripe bananas.

Page 6: In Scotland, a toddler tastes – and wears – chocolate.

Page 7: Two English schoolgirls stop for a spaghetti lunch.

Page 8: Young children in Hong Kong say grace before eating.

Page 9: These boys in Morocco, in northwest Africa, use their hands to eat couscous topped with vegetables and meat.

Page 10: Women on a trip to Antarctica eat lunch on their ship.

 **Page 11:** Children on a field trip to the George Washington Carver National Monument in Missouri, USA take a lunch break.

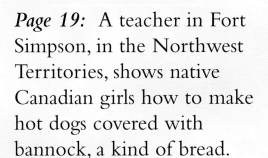 **Page 17:** Women in Ghana, a country in West Africa, make smoked herring on a grill.

 **Page 12:** A student on the go in Ho Chi Minh City, Vietnam, eats a quick snack.

 **Page 18:** At a shelter for homeless children in Bangkok, Thailand, children get a hot meal.

 **Page 13:** In Puttaparthi, India, a boy brings home a basket of tomatoes to cook.

 **Page 19:** A teacher in Fort Simpson, in the Northwest Territories, shows native Canadian girls how to make hot dogs covered with bannock, a kind of bread.

 **Page 14:** A teacher shows off the vegetables she has grown in Malawi, a country in southeastern Africa.

 **Page 20:** A child from the hills in Tamil Nadu, India, sits down to eat.

 **Page 15:** A woman in Nigeria, in West Africa, removes cocoa beans from their pods.

 **Page 21:** In Paris, France, a mother and son share some mealtime fun.

 **Page 16:** It's time to chop onions in this kitchen in Chisinau, Moldova.

A Note to Adults on Sharing This Book

Help your child become a lifelong reader. Read this book together, taking turns as you both read out loud. Look over the photographs and choose your favourites. Sound out new words and come back to them later for review. Then try these "extensions" – activities that extend the experience of reading and build discussion and problem-solving skills.

Talk about Eating

All around the world, you can find people eating. Discuss with your child the kinds of foods people eat in different countries. Where do you get the food you eat? Where do people in other parts of the world get their food? What ways of preparing food are shown in this book?

Make a Food Chart

With your child, draw pictures of the foods you both love to eat. Find pictures of your favourite foods in magazines. Then find out where they fit on the food pyramid. Which of your favourite foods should you eat less of – or more of – in order to be healthy?

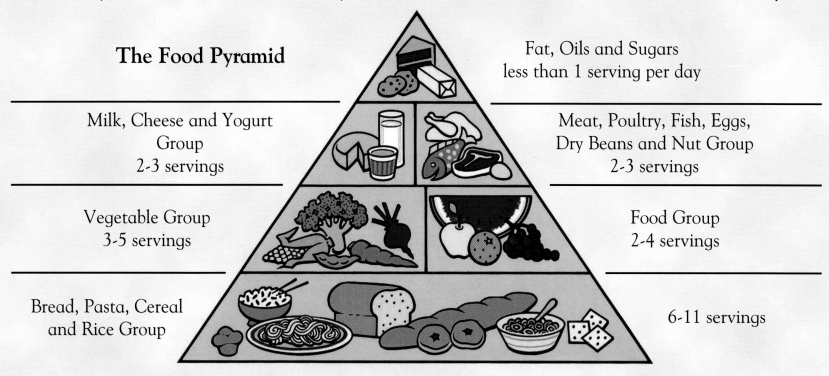

The Food Pyramid

Fat, Oils and Sugars
less than 1 serving per day

Milk, Cheese and Yogurt
Group
2-3 servings

Meat, Poultry, Fish, Eggs,
Dry Beans and Nut Group
2-3 servings

Vegetable Group
3-5 servings

Food Group
2-4 servings

Bread, Pasta, Cereal
and Rice Group

6-11 servings